Instant Zend Framework 2.0

Leverage the power of Zend Framework to build practical
MVC applications

A N M Mahabubul Hasan

BIRMINGHAM - MUMBAI

Instant Zend Framework 2.0

First published: August 2013

Production Reference: 1230813

Published by Packt Publishing Ltd.
Livery Place
35 Livery Street
Birmingham B3 2PB, UK.

ISBN 978-1-78216-412-8

www.packtpub.com

Credits

Author

A N M Mahabubul Hasan

Reviewer

Johann Bich

Acquisition Editor

Akram Hussain

Commissioning Editor

Mohammed Fahad

Technical Editor

Sharvari H. Baet

Copy Editors

Mradula Hedge

Brandt D'Mello

Project Coordinator

Romal Karani

Proofreader

Chrystal Ding

Production Coordinator

Kyle Albuquerque

Cover Work

Kyle Albuquerque

Cover Image

Sheetal Aute

About the Author

A N M Mahabubul Hasan is a Zend Certified Engineer, working professionally with Zend since 2006. He has completed his graduation in Computer Science & Engineering. He has been involved in numerous successful web development projects. Besides PHP, he has also been working heavily on Java and JavaScript. His Twitter handle is @uzzal.

I want to specially thank my brother-like friend, Milton Rodas, for his continuous support.

About the Reviewer

Johann Bich is a former web developer, working on both frontend and backend. After 7 years of PHP development (Zend Framework, Magento, and Prestashop) and frontend integration (HTML5, CSS3, and jQuery), he has redirected himself to the fields of requirement specification and project management, in which he successfully got his IPMA certification (Project management certification).

I would like to thank Mahabubul Hasan Uzzal for this book, and the opportunity he gave me to review it, the team at Packt Publishing for their help, and also my wife, for her support.

www.packtpub.com

Support files, eBooks, discount offers, and more

You might want to visit www.packtpub.com for support files and downloads related to your book.

Did you know that Packt offers eBook versions of every book published, with PDF and ePub files available? You can upgrade to the eBook version at www.packtpub.com and as a print book customer, you are entitled to a discount on the eBook copy. Get in touch with us at service@packtpub.com for more details.

At www.packtpub.com, you can also read a collection of free technical articles, sign up for a range of free newsletters and receive exclusive discounts and offers on Packt books and eBooks.

packtlib.packtpub.com

Do you need instant solutions to your IT questions? PacktLib is Packt's online digital book library. Here, you can access, read and search across Packt's entire library of books.

Why Subscribe?

- ✦ Fully searchable across every book published by Packt
- ✦ Copy and paste, print and bookmark content
- ✦ On demand and accessible via web browser

Free Access for Packt account holders

If you have an account with Packt at www.packtpub.com, you can use this to access PacktLib today and view nine entirely free books. Simply use your login credentials for immediate access.

Table of Contents

Instant Zend Framework 2.0

Welcome to *Instant Zend Framework 2.0*. This book has been especially created to provide you with all the information that you need to get set up with Zend Framework 2. You will learn its basics, get started with building your first course, and discover some tips and tricks for using Zend Framework 2.

This document contains the following sections:

So what is Zend Framework? helps you find out what Zend Framework actually is, what you can do with it, and why it's so great.

Installation explains how to download and install Zend Framework with minimum fuss and then set it up for quick use.

Quick start – creating your first web application will show you how to perform one of the core tasks of Zend Framework: creating a small address-book application and adding, editing, or deleting its contacts.

Top 5 features you need to know about will help you learn how to implement some important features, such as validating a form and logging into your application using Zend Framework.

People and places you should get to know provides you with many useful links to the project page and forums as well as a number of helpful tutorials, blogs, and Twitter feeds of Zend Framework's super contributors.

So, what is Zend Framework?

Throughout the years, PHP has become one of the most popular server-side scripting languages on the Internet. This is largely due to its steep learning curve and ease of use. However, these two reasons have also contributed to many of its shortcomings.

With minimal restrictions on how you write code with this language, you can employ any style or structure that you prefer, and thus it becomes much easier to write bad code.

But there is a solution: use a framework!

A framework simplifies coding by providing a highly modular file organization with code libraries of the most common scripting in everyday programming. It helps you develop faster by eliminating the monotonous details of coding and makes your code more re-usable and easier to maintain.

There are many popular PHP frameworks out there. A number of them have large, open source communities that provide a wide range of support and offer many solutions. This is probably the main reason why most beginner PHP developers get confused while choosing a framework.

I will not discuss the pros and cons of other frameworks, but I will demonstrate briefly why Zend Framework is a great choice.

Zend Framework (ZF) is a modern, free, and open source framework that is maintained and developed by a large community of developers and backed by Zend Technologies Ltd, the company founded by the developers of PHP.

Currently, Zend Framework is used by a large number of global companies, such as BBC, Discovery, Offers.com, and Cisco. Additionally, many widely used open source projects and recognized frameworks are powered by Zend Framework, such as in the case of Magento, Centurion, TomatoCMS, and PHProjekt. And lastly, its continued development is sponsored by highly recognizable firms such as Google and Microsoft.

With all this in mind, we know one thing is certain—Zend Framework is here to stay.

Zend Framework has a rich set of components or libraries and that is why it is also known as a component framework. You will find a library in it for almost anything that you need for your everyday project, from simple form validation to file upload. It gives you the flexibility to select a single component to develop your project or opt for all components, as you may need them.

Moreover, with the release of Zend Framework 2, each component is available via Pyrus and Composer. Pyrus is a package management and distribution system, and Composer is a tool for dependency management in PHP that allows you to declare the dependent libraries your project needs and installs them in your project for you.

Zend Framework 2 follows a 100 percent object-oriented design principle and makes use of all the new PHP 5.3+ features such as namespaces, late static binding, lambda functions, and closures.

Now, let's get started on a quick-start project to learn the basics of Zend Framework 2, and be well on our way to building our first Zend Framework MVC application.

Downloading the example code

You can download the example code files for all Packt books you have purchased from your account at `http://www.PacktPub.com`. If you purchased this book elsewhere, you can visit `http://www.PacktPub.com/support` and register to have the files e-mailed directly to you.

Installation

ZF2 requires PHP 5.3.3 or higher, so make sure you have the latest version of PHP.

We need a Windows-based PC, and we will be using XAMPP (`http://www.apachefriends.org/en/xampp.html`) for our development setup. I have installed XAMPP on my `D:` drive, so my web root path for my setup is `d:\xampp\htdocs`.

Step 1 – downloading Zend Framework

To create a ZF2 project, we will need two things: the framework itself and a skeleton application. Download both Zend Framework and the skeleton application from `http://framework.zend.com/downloads/latest` and `https://github.com/zendframework/ZendSkeletonApplication`, respectively.

Step 2 – unzipping the skeleton application

Now put the skeleton application that you have just downloaded into the web root directory (`d:\xampp\htdocs`) and unzip it. Name the directory `address-book` as we are going to create a very small address book application, or you can name it anything you want your project name to be. When you unzip the skeleton application, it looks similar to the following screenshot:

```
config
data
module
public
vendor
.gitignore
.gitmodules
composer.json
composer.phar
init_autoloader.php
LICENSE.txt
README.md
```

Step 3 – knowing the directories

Inside the `module` directory, there is a default module called `Application`. Inside the `vendor` directory, there is an empty directory called `ZF2`. This directory is for the Zend Framework library.

Unzip the Zend Framework that you have downloaded, and copy the `library` folder from the unzipped folder to the `vendor\ZF2` directory.

Step 4 – welcome to Zend Framework 2

Now, in your browser, type: `http://localhost/address-book/public`. It should show a screen as shown in the following screenshot. If you see the same screen, it means you have created the project successfully.

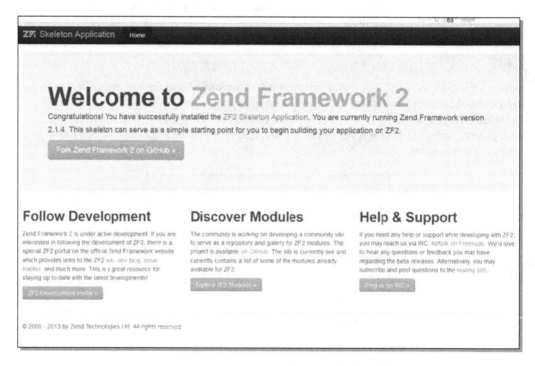

And that's it

By this point, you should have a working Zend Framework, and you are free to play around and discover more about it.

Quick start – creating your first web application

In this section, we will be creating a small address book application to demonstrate some basic functionality of Zend Framework, including the database **create, read, update, and delete** (**CRUD**) operation. In this small application, the user will be able to add new contacts and edit and delete contacts.

Step 1 – creating a module

Let's look again inside the `address-book` directory that we have created in the *Step 2 – unzipping the skeleton application* section. There is a `config` directory and inside that you will see an `autoload` directory and an `application.config.php` file. In this `application.config.php` file, we can tell the framework which modules to load and we can tell the paths where to look for those modules.

There is another directory called `module` where we will put all our custom modules. By default, there is an `Application` module in this directory; however, we are not going to use that. We will create our own custom module named `Contact`. To create a module, we need to do at least two things: first, create a directory called `Contact`. Second, inside that `Contact` directory, we need to add a `Module.php` file.

Let's create a `Contact` directory inside the module directory and the `Module.php` file inside that `Contact` directory. Now the `module` directory should look like the following:

```
/module
  /Contact
    Module.php
```

Add the following lines of code to the `Module.php` file:

```php
<?php
namespace Contact;

class Module{

}
```

And with that, we have just created our very first module.

Now we need to tell Zend Framework to load this `Contact` module. To do that, we need to add the following lines of codes in the `application.config.php` file:

```php
<?php
return array(
    'modules' => array(
        'Contact',
    ),
    'module_listener_options' => array(
        'module_paths' => array(
            './module',
        ),
    ),
);
```

Although we have now created and loaded our first module, it will not give us any output. If we browse to the URL `http://localhost/address-book/public`, it will give us an error because we have not created any controller and view yet.

Step 2 – creating a controller

If you look at the `Application` module that comes by default with the skeleton app, you will notice its directory structure is somewhat similar to the following code snippet:

```
/module
  /Application
      /config
            /module.config.php
      /src
            /Application
                    /Controller
                    /IndexController.php
      /view
      /Module.php
```

The `config` directory has a `module.config.php` file that holds all module-specific configurations such as `router`, `service_manager`, `controllers`, and `view_manager`. The `src` directory holds `Controllers` and `Models`, and the `view` directory holds all the view-related things; I will come back to this in the next step.

Let's create our first controller home for our `Contact` module, and for this we need to create the directory structure as follows:

```
/Contact
  /config
      /module.config.php
```

```
/src
    /Contact
            /Controller
                    /HomeController.php
            /Model
    /view
    /Module.php
```

Note that inside the `src` directory, we have the `/Contact/Controller` directory and inside that we have `HomeController.php`.

In ZF, the controller ends with the `Controller` suffix. So, as our controller name is `Home`, its class name should be `HomeController` and the filename should be the same as the class name. Our `HomeController.php` should look as follows:

```php
<?php
namespace Contact\Controller;
use Zend\Mvc\Controller\AbstractActionController;

class HomeController extends AbstractActionController
{
    public function indexAction()
    {
            echo 'Hello Zend Framework 2';
        return $this->response;
    }
}
```

Step 3 – configuring a controller

We have created our first controller in the last step; however, to make it work, we need to configure it in `config/module.config.php` and `Module.php`.

Add the following code in the `module.config.php` file:

```php
<?php
return array(
    'router' => array(
        'routes' => array(
            'home' => array(
                'type' => 'Zend\Mvc\Router\Http\Literal',
                'options' => array(
                    'route'    => '/',
                    'defaults' => array(
                        'controller' => 'Contact\Controller\Home',
                        'action'     => 'index',
                    ),
                ),
```

```
            ),
            'contact' => array(
                'type'    => 'Literal',
                'options' => array(
                    'route'    => '/contact',
                    'defaults' => array(
                        '__NAMESPACE__' => 'Contact\Controller',
                        'controller'    => 'Home',
                        'action'        => 'index',
                    ),
                ),

                'may_terminate' => true,
                'child_routes' => array(
                    'default' => array(
                        'type'    => 'Segment',
                        'options' => array(
                            'route'    =>
                            '/[:controller[/:action]]',
                            'constraints' => array(
                                'controller' =>

                             '[a-zA-Z][a-zA-Z0-9_-]*',
                                'action'        => '

                             '[a-zA-Z][a-zA-Z0-9_-]*',
                            ),
                            'defaults' => array(

                            ),
                        ),
                    ),
                ),
            ),
        ),
    ),
    'controllers' => array(
        'invokables' => array(
            'Contact\Controller\Home' =>

            'Contact\Controller\HomeController'
        ),
    ),
);
```

Add the following code in the `Module.php` file:

```php
<?php
namespace Contact;

use Zend\Mvc\ModuleRouteListener;
use Zend\Mvc\MvcEvent;

class Module
{
        public function onBootstrap(MvcEvent $e)
    {

        $eventManager = $e->getApplication()->getEventManager();
        $moduleRouteListener = new ModuleRouteListener();
        $moduleRouteListener->attach($eventManager);

    }

    public function getConfig()
    {
        return include __DIR__ . '/config/module.config.php';
    }

    public function getAutoloaderConfig()
    {
        return array(
            'Zend\Loader\StandardAutoloader' => array(
                'namespaces' => array(
                    __NAMESPACE__ =>
                            __DIR__ . '/src/' . __NAMESPACE__,
                ),
            ),
        );
    }
}
```

Now, in the browser go to the address book app `http://localhost/address-book/public`. You should see a page saying **Hello Zend Framework 2**.

Step 4 – creating a view

So far we have created and configured a controller, and now we will place all our view files inside the `view` directory of the `Contact` module. A view file has a close relation with the controllers. By default, every controller and action expects that there should be a corresponding view file for them. So this means if our controller name is `Home` and action name is `Index`, there should be a `.phtml` file in the `view` directory as follows:

```
/view
  /contact
    /home
      /index.phtml
```

For the view file, ZF uses the `.phtml` extension. Another important thing is that for showing all our application errors, we need to put the `.phtml` files in the error directory. We will create an `index.phtml` file for all general purpose errors and a `404.phtml` file for all page not found errors. So finally at this point, our view directory should be similar to the following code snippet:

```
/view
  /contact/
        /home
            /index.phtml
    /layout
        /layout.phtml
    /error
        /index.phtml
        /404.phtml
```

Let's add some code in these `.phtml` files. Add the following code in the `error/index.phtml` file:

```
<h1>An error occurred</h1>
<h2><?php echo $this->message ?></h2>
```

Add the following code in the `error/404.phtml` file:

```
<h1>Page not found</h1>
<h2><?php echo $this->message ?></h2>
```

Add the following code in the `home/index.phtml` file:

```
This is a view file of <b>(<?=$controller?>)</b> / (<?=$action?>).
```

Here, the value of the `$controller` and `$action` variable will come from the controller. I will show you how, in a moment, but before that let's talk about layouts.

Layout is a special kind of view that wraps the action's view; for example, in a normal website, you will see that the header and footer are common for every page. This doesn't mean they have written the header and footer in every single page. These common parts are normally written in layout. We will place a very basic `layout.phtml` file in the `layout` directory.

Let's add the following code in the `layout.phtml` file:

```php
<?php echo $this->doctype(); ?>
<html lang="en">
    <head>
        <meta charset="utf-8">
        <title>Address Book</title>
        <base href="<?=$this->basePath()?>/" />
    </head>
    <body>
        <h1>Address Book</h1>
         <hr />
        <div class="container">
            <?php echo $this->content; ?>
             <hr />
            <footer>
                <p>Address Book &copy; 2013</p>
            </footer>
        </div>
    </body>
</html>
```

Here in the code, the `<base>` tag is important because we have not created a virtual host, and our path is not directly under the web root directory. Also, the `$this->content;` function is important as it shows the action-specific view.

Now, let's configure all our view files with `view_manager` in the `module.config.php` file with the following code:

```php
<?php
return array(
    'router' => array(...),
    'controllers' => array(..),

        'view_manager' => array(
        'display_not_found_reason' => true,
        'display_exceptions'       => true,
        'doctype'                  => 'HTML5',
        'not_found_template'       => 'error/404',
        'exception_template'       => 'error/index',

        'template_map' => array(
            'layout/layout'        => __DIR__ . '/../view/layout/layout.
                                      phtml',

            'contact/home/index' => __DIR__ . '/../view/contact/home/
                                      index.phtml',

            'error/404'            => __DIR__ . '/../view/error/404.
                                      phtml',
```

```
            'error/index'        => __DIR__ . '/../view/error/index.
                                    phtml',

         ),
         'template_path_stack' => array(
             __DIR__ . '/../view',
         ),
      ),
   );
```

So view is now configured. To pass the value from the controller to a view file, we need to update the home controller's `indexAction` method with the following code:

```php
<?php
namespace Contact\Controller;

use Zend\Mvc\Controller\AbstractActionController;
use Zend\View\Model\ViewModel;

class HomeController extends AbstractActionController
{
    public function indexAction()
    {
        $data['action'] = __FUNCTION__;
        $data['controller'] = __CLASS__;
        return new ViewModel($data);
    }
}
```

Now let's browse the app again. Go to `http://localhost/address-book/public`, and you should see the output similar to the following screenshot:

Address Book

Add new Contact

This is a view file of (Contact\Controller\HomeController) / (indexAction).

Address Book © 2013

Step 5 – configuring a database

When working with a database, ZF is quite flexible; you can either use any third-party **Object Relational Mapper (ORM)** such as Doctrine or Propel, or you can use ZF's own DB library. However, here I will not show any of this because it is beyond the scope of this book. Rather, I will show you a different and easy way with PHP's native PDO library (http://php.net/manual/en/book.pdo.php) that most PHP developers are aware of.

Let's say we create a database named address_book_db. To configure this with the Contact module, open the module.config.php file, and add the following lines of code in the sevice_manager file:

```php
<?php
return array(
    'router' => array(...),
    'controllers' => array(..),
    'db' => array(
        'dsn' => 'mysql:dbname=address_book_db;host=localhost',
        'username' => 'your_db_username',
        'password' => 'your_password',
    ),
    'service_manager' => array(
        'factories' => array(
                'db_adapter' => function($sm) {
                $config = $sm->get('Config')['db'];

                    return new PDO( $config['dsn'],
                                    $config['username'],
                                    $config['password']);
                }
        ),
    ),
    'view_manager' => array(...),
);
```

Replace the db name if you have used a different name, and also your MySQL username and password. At this point, the database is configured. Now we can access this connection from any ServiceLocatorAware class in any module.

Step 6 – creating a model

Zend Framework does not prove a Zend\model component because model is just a simple class where we write all our business logic. That's why it is up to us to choose how we want it to work.

For this project, we will create a very basic model that will do CRUD operation using the PDO library. So let's create our first model inside the src/Contact/Model directory. We will name this model as Contact, so we need to create a Contact.php file inside the Model directory, and in this Contact.php file, we need to add the following code:

```php
<?php
namespace Contact\Model;

class Contact{
    private $_db;

    public function __construct($db) {
        $this->_db = $db;
    }
}
```

Note that in the code, the constructor has a $db argument. This is the PDO class instance. We will inject this PDO class instance from our Module class. To do this, we need to add the getServiceConfig method in the Module class as follows:

```php
public function getServiceConfig() {
        return array(
            'factories' => array(
                'Contact\Model\Contact' => function($sm) {
                    $db_adapter = $sm->get('db_adapter');
                    return new
                     \Contact\Model\Contact($db_adapter);
                }
            ),
        );
    }
```

Now, at this point, our model is fully capable of doing any kind of database operation with PDO. One of the ways to access this model from any controller is as follows:

```php
$contact = $this->getServiceLocator()->get('Contact\Model\Contact');
```

Step 7 – project in the big picture

So far we covered several configurations: how to create controller, model, and view, and how to connect with the database. Now we will see the project in the big picture.

Before we begin, let's create a table named `contact` using SQL as follows:

```
CREATE TABLE IF NOT EXISTS `contact` (
  `id` int(11) NOT NULL AUTO_INCREMENT,
  `name` varchar(50) NOT NULL,
  `email` varchar(50) NOT NULL,
  `phone` varchar(10) NOT NULL,
  PRIMARY KEY (`id`)
) ENGINE=InnoDB  DEFAULT CHARSET=latin1 AUTO_INCREMENT=1;
```

We will create our address book app's home page similar to this mockup layout:

Note that in the layout, we have the **Add new contact, Edit,** and **Delete** links. When a user clicks on the **Add new contact** link, we will take the user to the add new contact page, and after successful submission of the form, we will save the information and redirect the user to this home page and update the grid with the new row.

Again, if the user clicks on the **Edit** link, we will open that row in the edit contact page, just like the add new contact page; after successful submission of the form, we will update the information and redirect the user to this home page and update the row with the updated contact information. Clicking on the **Delete** link will not have any visual page; the user will just click on the link and it will take him to the controller and delete the row and redirect him to the home page with that row deleted.

The add and edit contact page will be similar to the following screenshot:

Let's start coding. First, open the Contact model that we created in the *Step 6 – creating a model* section. We will add a new getAllRows() method to it that will fetch all the rows from the contact table. Code for the getAllRows() method is as follows:

```
public function getAllRows() {
    $sql = "select * from contact";
    $stat = $this->_db->query($sql);
    return $stat->fetchAll();
}
```

Here in this method, the $this->_db instance is the PDO object, which we have injected in the contact model's constructor from the Module class.

Now open the HomeController class, and in the indexAction method, assign all the rows returned by the getAllRows() method to our view page. To do so, we need to update our indexAction method with the following code:

```
public function indexAction() {
    $contact = $this->getServiceLocator()
                        ->get('Contact\Model\Contact');
    $data['rows'] = $contact->getAllRows();
    return new ViewModel($data);
}
```

Now, open the `contact/home/index.phtml` file, and add the following code to view all the rows:

```
<div><a href="contact/home/new">Add new Contact</a></div>
<hr />
<div>
    <table>
        <tr>
            <th>Name</th>
            <th>Email</th>
            <th>Phone</th>
            <th>Action</th>
        </tr>
    <?php if(count($rows)>0):
        foreach($rows as $r):?>
        <tr>
            <td><?=$r['name']?></td>
            <td><?=$r['email']?></td>
            <td><?=$r['phone']?></td>
            <td><a href="contact/home/edit?id=<?=$r['id']?>">Edit</a>
                /
            <a href="contact/home/delete?id=<?=$r['id']?>">Delete</a>
            </td>
        </tr>
    <?php endforeach;endif;?>
    </table>
</div>
```

At this point, there are no data in the contact table. If we manually insert some data and browse to `http://localhost/address-book/public`, we will see an output as shown in the following screenshot:

Now we will create the add new contact form, and a `newAction` method in `homeController` and a `addRow` method in the `Contact` model.

Add the following code in the `newAction` method of `homeController`:

```
public function newAction(){
    if($_POST){
        $contact = $this->getServiceLocator()
                        ->get('Contact\Model\Contact');
        $contact->addRow($_POST);
        return $this->redirect()->toRoute('home');
    }

    return new ViewModel($_POST);
}
```

Here, `$this->redirect()` is a controller plugin. There are several other controller plugins like this; for example, `param`, `forward`, and `layout`.

What this redirect plugin does in this code is that after submission of the form, the `addRow()` method saves the data to the database and then redirects the plugin to do the redirection of the client to the home route. Remember, we have defined this home route in the `module.config.php` file's `router` section.

Let's create a `new.phtml` file in the `view/contact/home/` directory, and add the following code:

```html
<hr />
<div>
    <form method="post" action="new">
    Name <br />
    <input type="text" name="name" value="<?=$name?>" /><br />
    Email <br />
    <input type="text" name="email" value="<?=$email?>" /><br />
    Phone <br />
    <input type="text" name="phone" value="<?=$phone?>" /><br />
    <br /><br />
    <input type="submit" value="Save" />
    </form>
</div>
```

Now, open the `contact` model and add the `addRow` method to it as follows:

```
public function addRow($data){
    $sql = "INSERT INTO
            contact (name,email,phone)
            VALUES ('{$data['name']}',
                            '{$data['email']}',
                            '{$data['phone']}')";

    return $this->_db->exec($sql);
}
```

Now open `http://localhost/address-book/public/home/new`. You should see the new contact form. Fill up the form and click on the **Save** button. It will save the data to the database and redirect you to the home page with the new row showing.

The edit contact code is similar to the new contact code except that we need a to add a few extra lines of code; for example, the edit URL needs to carry the ID of the contact that we want to edit as shown in the following line of code:

```
contact/home/edit?id=<?=$r['id']
```

Then we need to fetch the contact row from the contact table and assign it to the edit contact form. So, we need a method such as `getRow($id)` that will return the row for `$id`.

Let's create the `getRow()` method in the `contact` model.

```
public function getRow($id) {
    $sql = "select * from contact where id=?";

    $stat = $this->_db->prepare($sql);
    $stat->execute(array($id));
    return $stat->fetch();
}
```

Also, we will need another method that will update the contact data. So we need to add an `updateRow()` method in this model as follows:

```
public function updateRow($data, $id) {
    $sql = "UPDATE contact SET
        name='{$data['name']}',
        email='{$data['email']}',
        phone='{$data['phone']}'
        WHERE id={$id}
        ";

    return $this->_db->exec($sql);
}
```

Now open the `homeController` file, and add a new `editAction` method to it as follows:

```
public function editAction(){
    $id = $this->params()->fromQuery('id',0);

    $contact = $this->getServiceLocator()
                        ->get('Contact\Model\Contact');

    if($_POST){
        $contact->updateRow($_POST, $id);
        return $this->redirect()->toRoute('home');
    }else{
        $row = $contact->getRow($id);
    }

    return new ViewModel($row);
}
```

Here, `$this->params()` is another controller plugin. So, what this edit action does is it takes the ID from the request URL and assigns it to the `$id` variable, and then fetches the row from the database based on that ID and assigns it to the `edit` view file. When the form is submitted, it saves the data to the contact table and redirects the user to the home route.

We need to add an `edit.phtml` file in the `view/contact/home/` directory, and add the following code to it:

```
<hr />
<div>
    <form method="post" action="edit?id=<?=$id?>">
    Name <br />
    <input type="text" name="name" value="<?=$name?>" /><br />
    Email <br />
    <input type="text" name="email" value="<?=$email?>" /><br />
    Phone <br />
    <input type="text" name="phone" value="<?=$phone?>" /><br />
    <br /><br />
    <input type="submit" value="Save" />
    </form>
</div>
```

Note that it is the same as the `new.phtml` file; the only difference is the `form` method's `action` URL.

The delete action is pretty straightforward. It will not have any view file, and it will just get the ID from the URL and delete the contact from the database using the contact model.

Code for the delete action is as follows:

```
public function deleteAction() {
    $id = $this->params()->fromQuery('id',0);

    $contact = $this->getServiceLocator()
                            ->get('Contact\Model\Contact');

    $contact->delRow($id);
    return $this->redirect()->toRoute('home');
}
```

Code for the delRow method of the Contact model is as follows:

```
public function delRow($id) {
    $sql = "delete from contact where id={$id}";
    return $this->_db->exec($sql); }
```

Top 5 features you need to know about

In the previous sections we have covered how to create a basic module with controller, model, and view and also how to inject the database connection to the model and the CRUD. Here in this section, we will dive deep into Zend Framework with some of its very common functionalities.

Input filter and validation

In the *Quick start – creating your first web application* section, we have created a `newAction` action and an `editAction` action. Both of these actions have one thing in common: they were dealing with the client's data. The client can insert anything which means they can insert malicious data that could lead to malicious attacks or invalidly formatted data; for example, we have a field for e-mail and e-mail has a specific format.

Zend Framework has a rich set of filters and validator classes (`Zend\Filter`, `Zend\Validator`, `Zend\InputFilter`). Here we will see how to filter and validate the client's data using `Zend\InputFilter`.

Let's update our `newAction` method in the `homeController` file with the following code:

```
public function newAction() {
    $invalids = array();
    $filter = array(
        'name' => array(
            'name' => 'name',
            'required' => true,
            'filters' => array(
                array('name' => 'StripTags'),
                array('name' => 'StringTrim')
            ),
            'validators' => array(
                array(
                    'name' => 'not_empty',
                ),
                array(
                    'name' => 'string_length',
                    'options' => array(
                        'min' => 3
                    ),
                ),
            ),
        ),
        'email' => array(
            'name' => 'name',
            'required' => true,
            'filters' => array(
                array('name' => 'StripTags'),
```

```
                array('name' => 'StringTrim')
            ),
            'validators' => array(
                array(
                    'name' => 'not_empty',
                ),
                array(
                    'name' => 'email_address',
                ),
            ),
        ),
        'phone' => array(
            'name' => 'name',
            'required' => true,
            'filters' => array(
                array('name' => 'StripTags'),
                array('name' => 'StringTrim')
            ),
            'validators' => array(
                array(
                    'name' => 'not_empty',
                ),
            ),
        ),
    );

    if ($_POST) {
        $factory = new \Zend\InputFilter\Factory();
        $input = $factory->createInputFilter($filter);
        $input->setData($_POST);

        if($input->isValid()){
            $contact = $this->getServiceLocator()
                        ->get('Contact\Model\Contact');

            $contact->addRow($_POST);
            return $this->redirect()->toRoute('home');
        }else{
            $invalids = $input->getInvalidInput();
        }

        $data = $input->getValues();
    }

    return new ViewModel(array('row'=>$data, 'invalids'=>$invalids));
}
```

In the `$filter` array, we have set filter and validator rules for each field; for example, for the name field, we have set two filters, `StripTags` and `StringTrim`, and two validators, `not_empty` and `string_length`.

As the name suggests, the `StripTags` filter removes any unwanted HTML tags, and `StringTrim` removes any unwanted space or newline character from the beginning and end of the given string.

Now we will activate our input filter using the `Zend\InputFilter\Factory` class and pass our input data to validate with the `setData` method.

If the inputs are valid, we will save the data in the database, or we will show error messages on the form view page. We will get all invalid inputs with the `getInvalidInput ()` method, and we will assign back our data and invalid inputs to the view page with the following code:

```
new ViewModel(array('row'=>$data, 'invalids'=>$invalids));
```

We have three fields in our form: `name`, `email`, and `phone`. If one of them is invalid or missing, the other field's value needs to stay there otherwise it will be annoying for the user to fill out the whole form every time one or more inputs are invalid.

Let's update our form view file (`new.phtml`) to show the error message as follows:

```
<hr />
<div>
    <div>
        <?php foreach($invalids as $err):
            $msgs = $err->getMessages();
            foreach($msgs as $m){
                echo '<div>'.$m.'</div>';
            }
        endforeach;?>
    </div>
    <form method="post" action="new">
    Name <br />
    <input type="text" name="name" value="<?=$row['name']?>" />
    <br />
    Email <br />
    <input type="text" name="email" value="<?=$row['email']?>" />
    <br />
    Phone <br />
    <input type="text" name="phone" value="<?=$row['phone']?>" />
    <br />
    <br /><br />
    <input type="submit" value="Save" />
    </form>
</div>
```

Now if we browse to this page and submit the form with invalid input(s), we should see errors as follows:

+ **Value is required and can't be empty**
+ **The input is less than 3 characters long**
+ **Value is required and can't be empty**
+ **The input is not a valid email address. Use the basic format local-part@hostname**
+ **Value is required and can't be empty**

We can use CSS to make these error messages more stylish.

Besides `StripTags` and `StringTrim`, Zend Framework has a few more standard filter classes such as `NumberFormat`, `PregReplace`, `StringToLower`, `Digits`, `Alpha`, and `Alnum`. You will find the full list of standard filter classes in the manual under the `Zend\Filter` package.

Just like filter classes, validator has many standard classes in Zend Framework such as `CreditCard`, `Date`, `Between`, `Digits`, `Identical`, `ISBN`, `InArray`, `Alnum`, and `Alpha`. You will find the full list of the standard validator classes in the manual under the `Zend\Validator` package.

You might be wondering why the `EmailAddress` class is written as `email_address`, or the `NotEmpty` class as `not_empty` in the validators' array. These are just class mappings, and you will find the full list of these names in the `Zend\Validator\ValidatorPluginManager`.php file's `$invokableClasses` array. Note that the array key doesn't have any underscore (_) because mapping will ignore any underscore character; for example, `not_empty` and `notempty` will mean the same.

View helper

In the last code example in the view page, we have printed the error messages using the following code:

```php
<?php foreach($invalids as $err):
    $msgs = $err->getMessages();
    foreach($msgs as $m){
        echo '<div>'.$m.'</div>';
    }
endforeach;?>
```

So, it will look really bad if we have many forms and we need to print the error messages with a repetitive code like this every time. Zend Framework has a good solution for this: we can create a View Helper for this repetitive code.

Basically, a helper is a class that implements at least `Zend\View\Helper\HelperInterface` and has a `setView` and `getView` method. Another way to create a custom view helper is by extending `Zend\View\Helper\AbstractHelper`. This `AbstractHelper` method implements `HelperInterface` giving you a head start in your development.

Let's create our very first custom view helper. We will call it `ErrorMsg`, and it will simply take an array and return a string. We will create our `ErrorMsg.php` file inside the `src/Contact/View/Helper` directory. So, our updated directory structure will now look as follows:

```
/Contact
  /config
  /src
      /Contact
              /Controller
              /Model
              /View
                    /Helper
  /view
        /contact
        /error
        /layout
  /Module.php
```

Code for our `ErrorMsg` helper class will be as follows:

```php
<?php
namespace Contact\View\Helper;

class ErrorMsg extends \Zend\View\Helper\AbstractHelper{
    public function __invoke($value){
        $msg = '';
        if(count($value)>0){
            foreach($value as $err){
                $msgs = $err->getMessages();
                foreach($msgs as $m){
                    $msg .= '<div>'.$m.'</div>';
                }
            }
        }
        return $msg;
    }
}
```

Now we have our `helper` class but to use this class on the view file, we need to register it. One way to do this is by adding a `getViewHelperConfig` method in the `Module` class as follows:

```
public function getViewHelperConfig() {
    return array(
        'invokables' => array(
            'error_msg' => 'Contact\View\Helper\ErrorMsg'
        ),
    );
}
```

Our helper is now fully ready to be used in the view file. Let's replace the previous error message showing code with the following line of code:

```
<?=$this->errorMsg($invalids);?>
```

This will show the error messages same as the previous code but is more clean. Let's see our final code for the `new.phtml` view file.

```
<hr />
<div>
    <div><?=$this->errorMsg($invalids)?></div>

    <form method="post" action="new">
    Name <br />
    <input type="text" name-"name" value="<?=$row['name']?>" /><br />
    Email <br />
    <input type="text" name="email" value="<?=$row['email']?>" />
    <br />
    Phone <br />
    <input type="text" name="phone" value="<?=$row['phone']?>" />
    <br />
    <br /><br />
    <input type="submit" value="Save" />
    </form>
</div>
```

Besides the custom view helper, Zend Framework has several built-in view helpers. Some of them are `BasePath`, `Cycle`, `Doctype`, `HeadLink`, `HeadMeta`, `HeadScript`, `HeadStyle`, `HeadTitle`, `InlineScript`, `JSON`, `Partial`, and `Placeholder`.

If you open the `view/layout/layout.phtml` file, you will see that we have already used `Doctype` and `BasePath` view helper in it as `<?php echo $this->doctype();?>` and `<?= $this->basePath()?>`.

Zend Log

We often need to log in to our apps for various reasons, such as debugging or error printing. We will see how we can use `Zend\Log` in this small app that we are building, but before we begin, let's see a few more points about `Zend\Log` as follows:

+ Most applications use the `Zend\Log\Logger` class's object the most. You can have as many logger objects as you like.

+ A logger object must contain at least one writer and can optionally contain one or more filters.

+ A writer is responsible for saving the data to storage.

+ A filter blocks the log data from being saved. A filter is applied to an individual writer. Filters can be chained.

+ A formatter can format the log data before it is written by a writer. Each writer has exactly one formatter.

Let's get started!

We will be introducing our logger in the `Module` class's `getServiceConfig` method. We will add another `Logger` element in the `factories` array as follows:

```
public function getServiceConfig() {
    return array(
        'factories' => array(
            ...
            'Logger' => function($sm) {
                $logger = new \Zend\Log\Logger;
                $writer = new \Zend\Log\Writer\Stream('data.log');

                $logger->addWriter($writer);
                return $logger;
            }
        ),
    );
}
```

Here in the code, our log filename is `data.log`, and it will be created in the application's root directory; you can also give the filename with the full path if you want. Our logger is ready to do any kind of logging, so let's do a test.

Add the following lines of code in the `HomeController`'s `indexAction` method.

```
$log = $this->getServiceLocator()->get('Logger');
$log->info('Hello Zend Log');
```

Now run the `indexAction` action by going to `http://localhost/address-book/public`. If everything went well, you should see a `data.log` file in the application's root path and in that file a line of text saying `'Hello Zend Log'`.

Zend EventManager

Zend Framework 2 introduces a new `EventManager` component. It allows a class to publish events that other objects can listen to and then act when the event occurs. This component is designed for the following cases:

- ✦ Implementing simple subject/observer patterns
- ✦ Implementing aspect-oriented designs
- ✦ Implementing event-driven architectures

The biggest advantage of using `EventManager` in our application is that we can decouple classes that really shouldn't be coupled together, which makes the code easier to write and maintain. In fact, this is so useful that Zend Framework 2's MVC system makes heavy use of `EventManager`.

Let's do some event handing in our small app. Suppose we call a function when a new contact is inserted, edited, or deleted. This means we will create an insert event, an edit event, and a delete event.

We will make our `Contact` model as an `EventManagerAware` class. To do this, we need to implement the `EventManagerAwareInterface` interface.

Let's open and update the `Contact` module with the following code:

```php
<?php

namespace Contact\Model;

use Zend\EventManager\EventManagerInterface;
use Zend\EventManager\EventManager;
use Zend\EventManager\EventManagerAwareInterface;

class Contact implements EventManagerAwareInterface {

    private $_db;
    protected $events;

    public function setEventManager(EventManagerInterface $events) {
        $events->setIdentifiers(array(
            __CLASS__,
            get_called_class(),
        ));
        $this->events = $events;
        return $this;
    }

    public function getEventManager() {
        if (null === $this->events) {
            $this->setEventManager(new EventManager());
```

```
        }
        return $this->events;
    }

    public function __construct($db) {
        $this->_db = $db;
    }

    public function getAllRows() {
        $sql = "select * from contact";
        $stat = $this->_db->query($sql);
        return $stat->fetchAll();
    }

    public function addRow($data){
        $this->getEventManager()->trigger('event.insert', $this);

        $sql = "INSERT INTO
            contact (name,email,phone)
            VALUES ('{$data['name']}','{$data['email']}','{$data['pho
                ne']}')";
            return $this->_db->exec($sql);
    }

    public function getRow($id) {
        $sql = "select * from contact where id=?";

        $stat = $this->_db->prepare($sql);
        $stat->execute(array($id));
        return $stat->fetch();
    }

    public function updateRow($data, $id) {
        $this->getEventManager()->trigger('event.edit', $this);
        $sql = "UPDATE contact SET
            name='{$data['name']}',
            email='{$data['email']}',
            phone='{$data['phone']}'
            WHERE id={$id}
            ";

        return $this->_db->exec($sql);
    }

    public function delRow($id){
        $this->getEventManager()->trigger('event.delete', $this);
        $sql = "delete from contact where id={$id}";
        return $this->_db->exec($sql);
    }
}
```

Take a detailed look at the code. Note that we have added two new methods, `setEventManager` and `getEventManager`, and the `Contact` class is implementing the `EventManagerAwareInterface` method, which also extends `EventsCapableInterface`. Here in the `Contact` module, `setEventManager` is a part of `EventManagerAwareInterface` and `getEventManager` is part of the `EventsCapableInterface` interface.

Then, look at the `addRow` method. Also, in the `updateRow` and `delRow` methods, we have triggered the events `event.insert`, `event.edit`, and `event.delete`. Whenever these methods are executed, they will trigger those events; if we call `addRow`, it will trigger the `event.insert` event, and if we call the `delRow` method, it will trigger the `event.delete` event. Now we need to attach a listening method to each of these events to do some actions. An event has no point without its listener.

We will add our event listeners in our `Module` class's `getServiceConfig` method where we will first instantiate the contact model. Let's update the previous code with the following one:

```
public function getServiceConfig() {
    return array(
        'factories' => array(
            'Contact\Model\Contact' => function($sm) {

                $db_adapter = $sm->get('db_adapter');
                $contact = new
                  \Contact\Model\Contact($db_adapter);
                $log = $sm->get('Logger');

                $eventManager = $contact->getEventManager();

                $eventManager->attach('event.insert',
                                function ($e) use ($log) {
                        $event = $e->getName();
                        $log->info("{$event} event
                                triggered");
                });

                $eventManager->attach('event.edit',
                                function ($e) use ($log) {
                        $event = $e->getName();
                        $log->info("{$event} event
                                triggered");
                });

                $eventManager->attach('event.delete',
                                function ($e) use ($log) {
                        $event = $e->getName();
                        $log->info("{$event} event
                                triggered");
```

```
                                });

                        return $contact;

                },
                'Logger' => function($sm) {
                    $logger = new \Zend\Log\Logger;
                    $writer = new \Zend\Log\Writer\Stream('data.log');

                    $logger->addWriter($writer);
                    return $logger;
                }
            ),
        );
    }
```

Now add a new contact, edit a contact, and delete a contact, and if everything went well, we will see the events in the log it prints as follows:

```
event.insert event triggered.
event.edit event triggered.
event.delete event triggered.
```

Uploading a file

File upload capability is very common in web applications. Zend Framework has a component (Zend\File\Transfer) to handle a file upload. Here I will show how to utilize this component for a file upload.

First, let's create another action method in our home controller. We will be naming it as fileUploadAction, and we will need to add a file-upload.phtml file in the /view/ contact/home directory. In the file-upload.phtml file, we will add code for an HTML form with enctype=multipart/form-data to handle the file upload. Let's create the code as follows:

```
<hr />
<div>
  <div><?php print_r($msg) ?></div>

    <form method="post" action="file-upload"
                    enctype="multipart/form-data">

    File <br />
    <input type="file" name="doc" />
    <br /><br />
    <input type="submit" value="Upload" />
    </form>
</div>
```

Here, `print_r($msg)` will print all kinds of messages and errors it will encounter when trying to upload the file. Our form's action is to upload the file using the home controller's `fileUploadAction` method.

Now lets see the code for the `fileUploadAction` method:

```
public function fileUploadAction() {

  if($this->getRequest()->isPost()){

        $adapter = new \Zend\File\Transfer\Adapter\Http();
        $adapter->setDestination('public/uploads');

        $files = $this->getRequest()->getFiles();

        if ($adapter->receive($files['doc']['name'])) {
              return new ViewModel(
              array('msg'=>$files['doc']['name'].' uploaded!')
              );
        }
    }
}
```

This is a very minimalistic code for a file upload. In this method, `Zend\File\Transfer\Adapter\Http` is the file transfer adapter class for the HTTP protocol. We have set our destination directory or the upload directory with the `setDestination()` method. We have set our destination path as `public/uploads`. So, we need to create an uploads directory inside the public directory of our application.

Here in the code, the `getFiles()` method returns the same value as the PHP's `$_FILES` variable.

Let's go a little deeper in the file upload. In the previous version of the code, we didn't validate what kind of file we should be uploading or what should be the size of the file. To do this, Zend Framework has various kinds of file validator class in the `Zend\Validator` component; for example, `Crc32`, `Extension`, `Hash`, `ImageSize`, `IsImage`, `IsCompressed`, `Size`, and `WordCount`.

Suppose we want to allow only PDF-type files of size 10 KB to 10 MB to be uploaded. For this, we need to update our previous `fileUploadAction` method with this code:

```
public function fileUploadAction() {

  if($this->getRequest()->isPost()){

      $size = new \Zend\Validator\File\Size(
                  array('min' => '10kB', 'max' => '10MB')
                  );

      $ext = new \Zend\Validator\File\Extension('pdf');

      $files = $this->getRequest()->getFiles();

      $adapter = new \Zend\File\Transfer\Adapter\Http();
      $adapter->setValidators(array($size,$ext));

      $adapter->setDestination('public/uploads');

      if($adapter->isValid()){
          if ($adapter->receive($files['doc']['name'])) {
              return new ViewModel(
                  array('msg'=>$files['doc']['name'].'
                      uploaded!')
                  );
          }
      }else{
          return new ViewModel(
              array('msg'=>$adapter->getMessages())
              );
      }
  }
}
```

Here in the code, we have added two validators with the `setValidators` method; one validator is to check the PDF extension and another one is to check whether the size of the file is between 10 KB to 10 MB.

If the file is valid, it will upload the file to the destination directory.

Like the validators, Zend Framework also provides some file filter classes; for example, `Encrypt`, `Lowercase`, `Uppercase`, and `Rename`. We can add these filter classes with the `setFilters` method on the adapter class instance just as we did for the `setValidators` method.

People and places you should get to know

Zend Framework is huge. To cover every aspect of the framework is beyond the scope of this book; hence, it is worthwhile to check the following links.

Once you have understood the basics of the framework, here are some more resources you should find very helpful:

- Official home page: `http://framework.zend.com`
- API documentation: `http://framework.zend.com/docs/api`
- Reference guide: `http://zf2.readthedocs.org/en/latest`
- ZF2 packages: `https://packages.zendframework.com`
- ZF2 modules: `http://modules.zendframework.com`
- Github repository: `https://github.com/zendframework/zf2`
- Webinars: `http://www.zend.com/en/resources/webinars/framework`
- IRC: `http://www.zftalk.com/channel`
- Mailing list: `http://framework.zend.com/archives`
- User groups: `http://framework.zend.com/participate/user-groups`
- Featured blogs: `http://framework.zend.com/participate/blogs`

We can follow the following contributors to gain more knowledge:

- Rob Allen
  - Blog: `http://akrabat.com`
  - Twitter: `@akrabat`
- Matthew Weier O'Phinney
  - Blog: `http://www.mwop.net/blog.html`
  - Twitter: `@mwop`
- Evan Coury
  - Blog: `http://blog.evan.pro`
  - Twitter: `@EvanDotPro`
- Abdul Malik Ikhsan
  - Blog: `http://samsonasik.wordpress.com`

About Packt Publishing

Packt, pronounced 'packed', published its first book "*Mastering phpMyAdmin for Effective MySQL Management*" in April 2004 and subsequently continued to specialize in publishing highly focused books on specific technologies and solutions.

Our books and publications share the experiences of your fellow IT professionals in adapting and customizing today's systems, applications, and frameworks. Our solution based books give you the knowledge and power to customize the software and technologies you're using to get the job done. Packt books are more specific and less general than the IT books you have seen in the past. Our unique business model allows us to bring you more focused information, giving you more of what you need to know, and less of what you don't.

Packt is a modern, yet unique publishing company, which focuses on producing quality, cutting-edge books for communities of developers, administrators, and newbies alike. For more information, please visit our website: www.packtpub.com.

Writing for Packt

We welcome all inquiries from people who are interested in authoring. Book proposals should be sent to author@packtpub.com. If your book idea is still at an early stage and you would like to discuss it first before writing a formal book proposal, contact us; one of our commissioning editors will get in touch with you.

We're not just looking for published authors; if you have strong technical skills but no writing experience, our experienced editors can help you develop a writing career, or simply get some additional reward for your expertise.

Zend Framework 1.8 Web Application Development

ISBN: 978-1-84719-422-0   Paperback: 380 pages

Design, develop, and deploy feature-rich PHP web applications with this MVC framework

1. Create powerful web applications by leveraging the power of this Model-View-Controller-based framework

2. Learn by doing – create a "real-life" storefront application

3. Covers access control, performance optimization, and testing

4. Best practices, as well as debugging and designing discussion

Expert PHP 5 Tools

ISBN: 978-1-84719-838-9   Paperback: 468 pages

Proven enterprise development tools and best practices for designing, coding, testing, and deploying PHP applications

1. Best practices for designing, coding, testing, and deploying PHP applications – all the information in one book

2. Learn to write unit tests and practice test-driven development from an expert

3. Set up a professional development environment with integrated debugging capabilities

4. Develop your own coding standard and enforce it automatically

Please check **www.PacktPub.com** for information on our titles

Zend Framework 2.0 by Example: Beginner's Guide

ISBN: 978-1-78216-192-9   Paperback: 228 pages

A step-by-step guide to help you build full-scale web applications using Zend Framework 2.0

1. Master application development with Zend Framework 2.0

2. Learn about Zend Framework components and use them for functions such as searching, image processing, and payment gateway integrations

3. Integrate third-party services for media sharing and payment processing

PHP Application Development with NetBeans: Beginner's Guide

ISBN: 978-1-84951-580-1   Paperback: 302 pages

Boost your PHP development skills with this step-by-step practical guide

1. Clear step-by-step instructions with lots of practical examples

2. Develop cutting-edge PHP applications like never before with the help of this popular IDE, through quick and simple techniques

3. Experience exciting features of PHP application development with real-life PHP projects

Please check **www.PacktPub.com** for information on our titles